Title:digital wealth formula: insider strategies

Richard T. Trojan

Why you need digital wealth formula

There is no shortage of wisdom among investing professionals about the methods you should use to generate wealth, such as saving for college, analyzing exchange-traded funds, and determining how long your money will endure.

These are the kinds of mathematical-plus-analytical insights that you would hire a smart financial manager to comprehend on your behalf. They include, among other things, modeling based on inflation rates, rates of return, and the percentage of equities vs. bonds. Unless you absolutely want to delve into the weeds, you shouldn't need to learn the mechanics of algorithms.In my experience, there is a much simpler formula for accumulating wealth that does not necessitate a graduate degree to comprehend. The following must be true in order to properly acquire and keep wealth:

•**Money**

• **Time**

• **Plan Strength**

 • **Discipline > Poor Decisions**

There's a rationale for all of the multiplication in this formula. If any of the variables representing the four crucial factors — money, time, plan strength, or discipline — equal zero, the formula's output will likewise be zero, and you will not be successful.

The obvious factors are money and time; the more money you invest and the longer you leave it invested, the better your odds. The quality of your strategy is also vital, which is why it's critical to work with a financial manager who understands your situation and aspirations.

However, the fourth essential, discipline, might mean the difference between simply "making ends meet" in retirement and leaving a legacy that secures your family's security for future generations. If you are not disciplined in your approach, you will end up with no wealth.

Remember that any number multiplied by zero equals zero.

When financial managers discuss discipline, we mean trust, intentionality, and focus:

Investors must have faith in the investment strategy and the planner's ability to stay on top of the markets, the economy, and the prognosis for each customer.

Investors must be deliberate in executing the strategy, living within its limitations, and recognizing changing life situations that may change the outlook.

Investors must concentrate on what they can manage rather than what they cannot, keeping the larger picture in mind as the market fluctuates over time.

As with any other human endeavor, the most successful people are those who have the discipline to stick to their strategy in order to achieve their objectives. They are well acquainted with themselves and are always truthful with themselves.

Every wealth manager has a roster of former clients who refused to listen, who believed they knew better than their financial advisor because they heard about a hot tip, an IPO, or the latest trend in get-rich-quick trading. (In reality, several of their ideas are just fancier-sounding copies of Beanie Babies and baseball cards).

You pay your wealth manager to execute a job for you, but you also have a role to play. Emotions can obscure people's judgment when it comes to money, and without discipline, even the best-laid plans can fail.

This takes us to the harsh reality: money does not equal intelligence. Don't mix riches with wealth — or intelligence with intelligence.

It is true that being intelligent can help you make money. Being born into a wealthy family, on the other hand, can be advantageous. Money alone does not equate to riches, and if it is not treated with a disciplined approach — one that takes emotion from the process — it will be transitory.

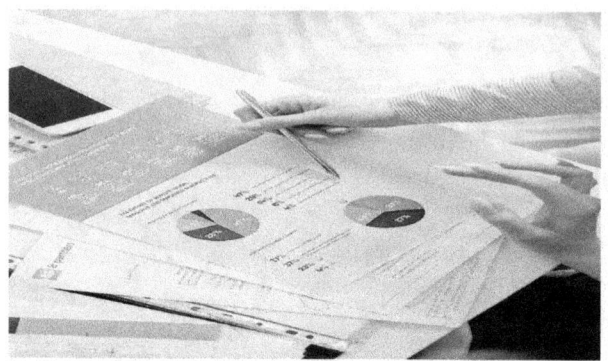

CHAPTER 1

Mastering the Digital Landscape

products or services. Affiliates are paid for each sale made as a result of their referral.

Analytics and data analysis are essential for measuring the efficiency of your **digital marketing operations.** Google Analytics, for example, gives valuable information on website traffic, user behavior, and conversion rates.

Developing a Comprehensive Digital Marketing Strategy

Email Marketing: You may engage with your audience on a more personal level by using this direct contact channel. Effective email marketing can nurture leads, promote products, and drive conversions.

Pay-Per-Click (PPC) advertising: PPC campaigns, which are commonly conducted on platforms such as Google advertising or social media, allow you to display advertising to individuals based on keywords, demographics, and behaviors that you specify. Because you only pay when someone clicks on your ad, it is a low-cost method of increasing visitors.

The process of cooperating with individuals or businesses to promote your products or services is known as affiliate marketing. Affiliates are paid for each sale made as a result of their referral.

Analytics and data analysis are essential for measuring the efficiency of your **digital marketing operations.** Google Analytics, for example, gives valuable information on website traffic, user behavior, and conversion rates.

Developing a Comprehensive Digital Marketing Strateg

A good digital marketing strategy integrates multiple components, utilizing the strengths of each channel to create a coherent and compelling brand experience. The first step is to understand your target audience's needs and internet behavior. You may then tweak your content and messaging to appeal to your target demographic across several platforms.

Accepting Adaptability and Agility

One of the most significant advantages of digital marketing is the ability to pivot and react in real time. Metrics and performance are tracked on a regular basis.

 regular basis allows you to fine-tune your methods for better results. This adaptable approach keeps you ahead of market trends and consumer preferences.

Now that we've covered the important components of a great internet business strategy, let's put it all together

Setting Objectives: Providing Clarity and Direction

To begin, it is necessary to define your objectives. Setting specific goals, such as increasing income by 20% or obtaining 100 new clients, aids in providing focus and a clear path to follow. By expressing your goals, you get clarity and can better focus your efforts to achieve them.

Creating a Mission Statement to Communicate the Purpose of the Company

A mission statement conveys what your organization stands for in a single sentence. It embodies your company's basic values and serves as a guiding principle. For example, a mission statement could be "to inspire healthier communities" or "to provide fun spaces for everyday fitness." Creating an effective mission statement allows you to communicate the purpose and values of your firm to internal and external stakeholders.

Defining Your Unique Selling Proposition (USP):

Making Yourself Stand Out from the Crowd

It is vital to identify your unique selling point (USP) in order to differentiate yourself from competitors in the online market. Investigate similar businesses and conduct comprehensive research to determine what sets you apart. Excellent customer service, new product features, or a specific market that you serve could be your unique selling point. Understanding your unique selling proposition (USP) enables you to capitalize on your strengths and stand out in a crowded environment.

Setting and Achieving Specific Objectives

Once you've determined your objectives, it's time to act. Here are some specific goals and methods for achieving them:

a. Increase Sales: Driving traffic to your website is essential for making online sales. Experiment with numerous tactics such as paid advertising, search engine optimization (SEO), and content marketing to bring more people to your site and convert them into consumers.

b. Increase Brand Awareness: Social media platforms help current and prospective customers become more familiar with brands. Engage your target audience, explain your brand's principles and personality, and post relevant content that they will find interesting.

c. Build Your Email Marketing List: To expand your email marketing list, offer incentives and emphasize the value members will receive. Give customers compelling reasons to join and stay connected with your firm, whether it's exclusive content, discounts, or member-only updates.

Creating a Profitable Online Strategy

Now that we've covered the fundamental components of a great internet business strategy, let's go through how to put it all together.

a. Define the company's goal: Define the overarching goal you hope to achieve with your web strategy.

b. Develop a mission statement: Develop a mission statement that summarizes your company's purpose and beliefs.

C. Identify the company's USP: Identify the unique selling point that distinguishes you from competitors.

Companies must have an effective online business plan in order to succeed in the digital landscape. Setting objectives, establishing a mission statement, and identifying a unique selling point will help you stand out and guide your efforts toward achieving your business goals. Set specific goals and implement strategies to boost sales, raise brand exposure, and expand your email marketing list. You'll be on the road to online success and long-term growth with a well-crafted online plan.

Creating an Online Presence

You may develop a strong online presence by creating a small business website. With the majority of consumers using the internet to find products and services, having a website guarantees that your company is discoverable and available to potential clients. It functions as a virtual storefront, displaying information about your services, contact information, and more.

You can reach a worldwide audience by establishing an online presence that extends your reach beyond the local neighborhood. This opens up new avenues for growth and expansion, allowing you to interact with clients from various locations and even other nations.

Increasing Your Reach

One of the key benefits of a small business website is the potential to reach a larger audience. Unlike traditional brick-and-mortar establishments, which are geographically limited, an online presence allows you to connect with customers from all over the world.

You may boost your visibility and acquire a larger consumer base by using successful digital marketing tactics such as search engine optimization (SEO) and social media marketing. You may increase your search engine results and drive organic traffic to your website by optimizing your website for relevant keywords. Check out our article on seo for small company websites to discover more about SEO for small business websites.

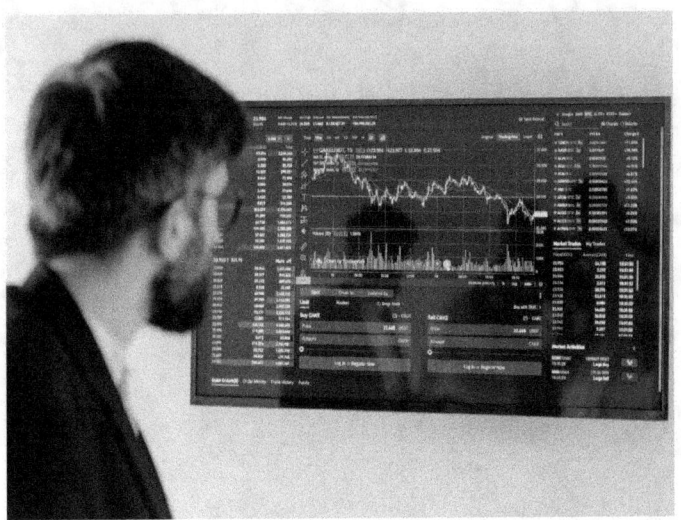

CHAPTER 2

Navigating Online Marketplaces

- It conducts extensive research on numerous internet marketplaces once you have a clear idea of your business objectives. **Some popular choices are:**

Amazon: is ideal for businesses of all sizes because of its large client base and fulfillment capabilities.

Shopify: A comprehensive e-commerce platform for creating and customizing your own online store.

eBay: A large range of product categories makes it suitable for both consumer and business-to-business transactions.

Etsy: A marketplace for handmade, antique, and craft items aimed towards creative entrepreneurs.

Alibaba: is primarily concerned with facilitating business-to-business transactions, particularly for sourcing products from overseas.

Consider marketplace costs, seller support, audience demographics, seller reputation, and any platform-specific features or tools. Reading reviews and speaking with other vendors who have experience with various marketplaces might provide useful information.

Recognize Marketplace Fees and Policies

Fees are usually charged by online markets to cover operational costs and to offer important services. It's critical to fully comprehend the pricing structures and rules of each platform you're considering. Consider listing costs, transaction fees, subscription fees, and any additional expenses for marketing or promotional features.

Also, learn about the marketplace's policies on shipping, returns, customer support, and intellectual property rights. These rules can have a big impact on your company's operations and customer experience, so be sure they are consistent with your business model and values.

Determine the target audience and reach

Your business's success on an online marketplace is primarily reliant on the platform's intended demographic and reach. Consider the marketplace's geographical breadth, the demographics of its user population, and whether it aligns with your target clients. Some platforms are more global in scope, while others are more focused on certain regions or countries.

Examine the market's marketing and promotion capabilities as well. Is it possible to use it to promote your products or services? Can you use its existing client base to boost your brand's visibility? Examining these characteristics will assist you in determining the platform that will most successfully reach and engage your target audience.

Consider Seller Support and Resources

Selling on an online marketplace can be difficult at times, especially if you're unfamiliar with the platform or e-commerce in general. Look for marketplaces with strong seller support and resources. Educational resources, forums or communities, dedicated customer support, and access to analytical tools or reports are all examples of this. A platform that provides comprehensive support can help you optimize your business operations, resolve difficulties quickly, and keep current on industry trends.

Improve Your Listings

Optimizing your listings is necessary for increasing the visibility of your products. This includes producing high-quality product photos and descriptions, employing pertinent keywords and tags, and providing competitive pricing and shipping alternatives. CommerceJet provides listing optimization services to businesses in order to assist them enhance their visibility and acquire more clients.

Inventory and Order Management

Managing inventories and orders efficiently is critical to success on online marketplaces. This includes keeping track of inventory levels, updating listings as things sell out or return to stock, and establishing shipping and return procedures. CommerceJet provides inventory management and order fulfillment services to assist businesses in streamlining these processes and focusing on sales growth.

CHAPTER 3

Building Profitable Online Ventures

Building a successful online business takes a lot of time and effort. Choosing an idea that matches your abilities and interests will therefore boost your chances of success and make the journey worthwhile.

The 30 most profitable online businesses to consider are listed below.

1. Work as a Freelancer

Earnings are estimated to be around $33/hour, depending on the industry and area.

Skills and experience in a specific field are required.

The emergence of the gig economy has made freelancing a viable alternative to traditional 9-to-5 occupations. In fact, 75% of freelancers reported higher earnings than their previous full-time job.

Those with prior work experience might use their expertise and network to launch a respected freelance firm.

You can work as a freelancer in almost any field. Web developers, graphic designers, and writers, on the other hand, are among the most in-demand careers online.

To begin your free online business idea, choose a specialty and a distinctive selling point to differentiate yourself in a competitive market. Elise Dopson, for example, is a freelance writer who specializes in writing journalistic-style content for B2B and SaaS organizations.

To promote their services online, freelancers typically construct a portfolio website. Signing up for freelance markets such as Fiverr and building a LinkedIn profile can also help to boost your internet presence.

2. Begin a site Estimated monthly income: $100-$10,000+, depending on site running costs and monetization channels

Writing, content marketing, and search engine optimization (SEO) abilities are required.

One of the most profitable online business ideas is to start a blog. Many six-figure entrepreneurs, such as Pat Flynn, began by blogging to a limited audience about their abilities and knowledge.

A successful blogging business entails more than just sharing opinions on a topic. Before you create a blog, keep the following points in mind:

Niche. A website that focuses on a single topic is more effective than one that covers a variety of themes. For inspiration, read our blog ideas page.

The standard of the content. Producing original and high-quality material can convert visitors into loyal readers and help your blog rank better on search engine results pages.

Size of the traffic. Bloggers who have a large number of visitors have a higher opportunity of recruiting new business partners and selling their products or services.

Options for monetization. Affiliate marketing, Google Ads, and sponsored content are all popular ways to make money with a blog. Consider combining them to increase your revenues.

3. Create and self-publish an eBook

Estimated earnings: 35-75% of the eBook's price, depending on the platform.

Creative writing and content marketing skills are required.

To become an author, you no longer need to submit a manuscript to a publisher. Anyone with a personal website or self-publishing sites like Amazon KDP and Apple Books can sell eBooks.

eBooks are ideal for collecting current content into a comprehensive guide if you're a blogger. Elna Cain does this with her long-form essays. She also provides downloadable worksheets in the eBooks to increase the product's value.

Self-publishing platforms provide the advantage of an existing audience, saving you the time and effort of starting from scratch. You cannot, however, collect the eBook's gross earnings. As a result, many writers construct a website in order to maximize their earnings.

If you decide to create one, read our lesson on how to design your own website from start.

Keep in mind that the cost of self-publishing a book ranges from $150 to $2,000. So, if you want to pursue an internet venture, make sure to pay for the first fees.

4. Launch an Online Store

Estimated annual income: $1,000-$100,000+, depending on the eCommerce business, its expenses, and the size of the market.

Business management, internet marketing, and site maintenance skills are required.

One of the best small business ideas is to start an eCommerce store to sell clothes or other things. Investigate trendy products or enter a micro niche to generate online store ideas. Although specialty segmentation may initially attract low traffic levels, it helps lessen competition and provides significant development potential.

Neuro, a firm that makes caffeinated gum and mints, is an outstanding example of a successful micro-niche business. The product was established by the inventors to be a healthy alternative to energy drinks and coffee.

Before you launch your online store, thoroughly assess the initial costs. The cost of developing a website is determined by a variety of factors, including its features and platform.

A simple small business website may cost between $100 and $500. However, if the eCommerce site is large and intricate, the cost may be $10,000 or more.

Consider selling on social media platforms such as Facebook or Instagram in addition to your eCommerce website. Diversifying your sales channels will help you reach a larger audience and enhance your revenue.

5. Launch a Dropshipping Company

Estimated monthly income: $200-$3,000+, depending on the size of the internet store and the market.

Business management, internet marketing, and site maintenance skills are required.

Dropshipping is one of the easiest companies for novices to start because it is low-risk but rewarding.

This business model entails collaborating with suppliers to offer their items through your platform. The vendor is in charge of storage and shipment, while the seller is in charge of marketing the items to potential buyers.

Because there is no need to manage inventories, the initial expenses are low. The average cost of launching a dropshipping website is $150. This amount includes a web hosting service, a domain name, and a Sprocket supplier directory membership.

Customers' trust is essential to the success of this small business model because they cannot inspect the products in person. To avoid problems, evaluate suppliers before collaborating, and provide outstanding customer service to assure their contentment.

6. Thrifted Goods Flipping and Selling

Estimated monthly salary: $50-$5,000+ Requirements: business management and negotiation skills

Sell secondhand products online for a profit if you're seeking a low-cost online business concept. Look for unused items of good quality around your house or buy used stuff from second hand stores.

Then, look up how much competitors charge for their products to estimate their prices. Repairing or recycling the item may be necessary in some circumstances to boost its value. While not required, having basic handyman or making abilities is advantageous in this sector.

For example, finest dressed, a fashion YouTuber, restored thrifted clothing and sold them on the fashion marketplace Depop.

7. Market Handmade Items

Estimated annual income: $30,000+, depending on materials and time spent manufacturing the product.

Artisanal or handicraft abilities are required.

The internet has helped artisans' craftsmanship appeal to the business sector through things to manufacture and sell.

Unlike merchants who work with suppliers, you can sell unique items that customers cannot find anywhere else. As a result, charging more for your creations is an option.

Bridget Bodenham is one of many artists who make a living by selling their work. She designs and sells vase sets via an eCommerce website, allowing her complete control over the brand's operations and marketing initiatives.

Selling on Etsy is another option. Etsy, which has over 96 million shoppers globally, may help you target ideal customers and grow a following. However, be prepared to compete for the attention of buyers with other merchants.

8. Sell Prints Earn an estimated 10-20% commission each print.

Artistic abilities such as photography, graphic design, and fine arts are required.

Print sales are one of the best business ideas for visual artists. You can earn money and promote your art by displaying it in people's homes.

Making an online store and signing up with an on-demand printing service like Printful is one of the simplest methods to sell prints.

This strategy allows you to create more artwork while focusing on marketing the business. Meanwhile, the printing service handles the ordering and shipment.

A Beautiful Mess, for example, sells full-size digital versions of their works. Customers can then print and frame your artwork themselves, saving on shipping expenses.

However, be aware of anyone who duplicates the files. Include a copyright notice with each piece of art and take action if there is infringement.

9. Work as an Affiliate Marketer

Estimated income: $50,000 per year, based on affiliate program and theme.

Requirements: abilities in content marketing

Affiliate marketing is one of the most cost-effective internet business opportunities. A brand's products or services are promoted by an affiliate marketer by putting links to them in their content. They will be compensated based on the amount of purchases completed via the affiliate link.

Sign up for affiliate programs such as Amazon Associates, Skimlinks, or Hostinger Affiliates to get started with this web business.

Then, create content, such as blog entries, that contains information on the products to which you're linking. The idea is to generate unique material that is relevant to the readers' interests.

Baby Gear Lab, a site dedicated to child care essentials, is a good affiliate website example. It provides detailed baby product recommendations and reviews.

The Baby Gear Lab blog also includes affiliate disclaimers, which inform readers that the website's owner will receive compensation if they utilize the links to purchase products.

CHAPTER 4

The Power of Digital Marketing

Businesses in this fast-paced digital era are continuously looking for new methods to stay relevant and connect with their target audience. Enter digital marketing, a game-changing concept that has transformed how businesses promote their goods and services. This blog will go into the realm of digital marketing, its numerous components, and why organizations must embrace this powerful tool in order to thrive in the online marketplace.

What exactly is digital marketing?

Digital marketing refers to a variety of online strategies used to reach, engage, and convert prospective customers. Unlike traditional marketing tactics, digital marketing effectively connects with target consumers through digital channels like search engines, social media platforms, websites, email, and mobile apps. Its primary goal is to create leads, drive website traffic, raise brand visibility, and eventually increase conversions.

Digital Marketing Elements:

SEO (Search Engine Optimization): SEO is an important part of digital marketing that focuses on improving websites to improve their exposure and rankings on search engine results pages (SERPs). Businesses may improve their organic search ranks, bring targeted traffic to their websites, and create their online authority by utilizing numerous tactics such as keyword research, on-page SEO, and link building.

Content Marketing: In the world of digital marketing, content reigns supreme. material marketing entails generating and disseminating valuable, relevant, and consistent material in order to attract and engage a certain target audience. This can include blog entries, articles, videos, infographics, and other types of content. Businesses may identify themselves as industry thought leaders, create trust, and cultivate long-term client relationships by delivering quality content.

With billions of active users, social media platforms have become a goldmine for businesses looking to extend their online presence. Social media marketing entails using sites such as Facebook, Instagram, Twitter, and LinkedIn to promote products and services, interact with customers, and raise brand awareness. Businesses can reach a large audience, generate website traffic, and build meaningful connections with their customers by using the power of social media.

Pay-Per-Click (PPC) Advertising: PPC advertising is a type of paid advertising in which businesses pay a fee each time their ad is clicked. Platforms such as Google Ads and social media advertising networks enable businesses to construct highly focused ad campaigns in order to attract their ideal clients. Businesses may maximize their ROI and drive quality leads by carefully picking keywords, customizing ad copy, and monitoring campaign performance.

Email marketing is an excellent tool for developing client connections and increasing conversions, despite the rise of social media and other digital channels. Sending tailored, targeted emails to a segmented audience is what email marketing entails. Businesses can keep their customers informed, boost traffic to their website, promote special offers, and establish brand loyalty through well-crafted email campaigns.

The Importance of Digital Marketing: In today's digital age, consumers rely on the internet to study items, make purchasing decisions, and seek advice. Businesses who do not embrace digital marketing risk falling behind in a highly competitive industry. Businesses that use digital marketing methods can:

Extend their reach: With digital marketing, firms may tap into worldwide marketplaces and reach a larger audience beyond their local bounds.

Target targeted audiences: Businesses may accurately target their ideal clients through digital marketing based on demographics, interests, and online behavior, improving the possibility of conversions.

Results must be measured and analyzed: Unlike traditional marketing tactics, digital marketing enables accurate campaign tracking and analysis. Businesses can optimize their marketing strategy by measuring key performance indicators (KPIs), gaining insights, and making data-driven decisions.

Cost-effectiveness: Digital marketing is frequently found to be less expensive than traditional marketing strategies. Businesses may deliberately manage their money, test campaigns, and alter their plans in real-time, assuring the best return on investment.

CHAPTER 5

Monetizing Your Online Presence

Growing your social media following is one of the most effective ways to strengthen your personal brand, improve your online business, and benefit from business opportunities in general. However, as your social media presence grows, you may want to capitalize on it - and directly monetize it - rather than using it to supplement your other income streams.

Fortunately, there are numerous ways to monetize your social media presence, especially if you devote sufficient time and attention to it. Let's go over each of them in greater detail.

PARTICIPATE IN AN AFFILIATE MARKETING PROGRAM

To begin, you can enroll in an affiliate marketing program. "An affiliate marketing program requires you to directly promote products to your social media following or audience," explains Christy Pyrz, Chief Marketing Officer of Paradigm Peptides. For example, you could create a Facebook post highlighting the benefits of a specific product or a short and informative video demonstrating how you use the product in your daily life.

Then, in the social media post, you include an affiliate marketing link. "Whenever one of your followers clicks on the affiliate link and makes a purchase, you'll get a cut of the profits in the form of a commission percentage," Ryan Rottman, Co-Founder and

CEO of OSDB Sports, explains. "This makes it one of the best ways to generate passive income based solely on your social media following."

Affiliate marketing is extremely beneficial because it allows you to earn money from your social media posts, blog posts, and videos. All you need to do is include an affiliate link for each product you promote or advertise!

Even better, almost anyone can participate in an affiliate marketing program. Even if you don't yet have a large number of followers or a large social media presence, you can still join one of these programs and start earning money on the side, especially if your following increases concurrently.

COLLABORATE WITH BRANDING (BECOME AN INFLUENCER)

You may also monetize your social media presence by becoming an influencer. When you become an influencer, you partner with brands either publicly or subtly. In either scenario, you use your social media presence to:

Promote particular brands, bolstering their audience's brand recognition and market domination

Promote or advertise specific products with the purpose to drive sales for those things

Lead the debate in certain industries or niches to divert attention to various brands

And more

Partnering with brands is the ultimate goal for many social media influencers. However, realize that you won't always hit it rich right off the bat.

To become a highly rich influencer and actually monetize your social media presence, you'll need to build up your following over time. Sean Doherty, General Manager of Box Genie, adds, "A lot of important brands only partner with social media influencers who have massive audiences and personal brands that work with their own."

To partner with brands more successfully:

Be sure that you have a personal brand that you stick to throughout time, such as an aesthetic, sort of content you generate, etc.

Start small by collaborating with lesser brands to learn how to execute the work and how to speak to your audience to drive sales/conversions

MAKE AN ONLINE COURSE

You can also monetize your social media presence by creating an online course. If you have any skill and some ability to teach, you can use an online educational platform like Teachable to quickly and easily create and deliver courses to your audience members.

You can directly monetize these online courses by charging people to receive their materials. You can, however, monetize your social media presence with free courses by:

Using the courses as a vector to drive traffic to an online store (more on this later)

Using the courses as vectors to drive purchases of specific products - you can use this strategy in conjunction with the above-mentioned partnering with brands across multiple channels or avenues at the same time.

OFFER YOUR CONSULTANT SERVICES

Have extensive experience in social media marketing or other fields? You can use your social media presence to promote your consulting services.

"Say you have a lot of experience in digital marketing," says Alex Novak, CEO of SLR. You can add a tag or line at the end of each social media post stating that you are available for consulting services. Consultants can earn a lot of money, especially if their skills are in high demand or are uncommon."

To monetize your social media presence in this manner, you must, of course, have valuable skills. Nonetheless, leveraging your social media followers is the best way to get new clients if you have the right skills.

MARKET LEADS TO COMPANIES

Selling leads is one way to monetise your social media following. Individuals or potential clients who are interested in what you or another business is selling are referred to as leads. You can collect leads and sell them to other companies if you have a huge following with a special interest.

"For example, let's say you're a fitness influencer who enjoys sharing social media content about eating well and exercising," explains Max Schwartzapfel, CMO of Fighting For You. "As you build up your following, you can sell those leads to apparel companies, fitness companies, nutritional snack brands, and so on."

Selling leads to businesses may result in valuable influencer partnerships. According to Cody Candee, the Founder and CEO of Bounce Luggage Storage, "this highlights the potential of monetizing your social media presence in multiple ways at the same time."

FUNDS FOR CREATOR

Finally, depending on the social media networks you use the most, you may be eligible to join a so-called creator fund. TikTok, for example, has a creator fund that pays out to its most popular users.

"Essentially, if you build up a large enough following, your social media platforms will pay you to stay active and keep people engaged on the site," explains Sasha Ramani, Associate Director of Corporate Strategy at MPOWER Financing. The more people are engaged, the more likely they are to view adverts and make purchases, after all! However, this method is only possible if you have a significant following in the first place.

HOW MANY FOLLOWERS DO YOU NEED FOR MONETIZATION?

When it comes to monetizing your social media following, the more followers you have, the better. No brand wants to partner with would-be "influencers" who just have 500 or so followers.

If you actually want to start monetizing your followers, you need at least several thousand. Even then, that modest number of followers would only be ideal for particular monetization techniques, such as sending people to your online store.

Want to work with prominent businesses or earn some advertising deals? You'll need at least 50,000 followers on average to make your personal brand interesting to marketing companies. Depending on your niche, personality, and your influencing technique, this could take you anywhere from few months to many years.

"Fortunately, followers tend to snowball in number as you accumulate them," explains Omid Semino, CEO and Founder of Diamond Mansion. "It's harder to get your first 1000 followers than it is to go from 1000 followers to 10,000, for instance."

Bottom line: To maximize profitability of your social media presence, gather as many followers as you can before pursuing advertising or brand partnership partnerships.

CHAPTER 6

Investing in the Digital Age

Welcome, fellow digital explorers, to the thrilling world of digital investing! The days of dirty stock exchange floors and frantic phone calls to brokers are long gone. You can now delve headfirst into the fascinating world of making money online through stocks and trading with only a few clicks and a dash of online savvy. So put on your virtual helmets and prepare for a crazy ride!

The opportunities for financial success and empowerment have grown dramatically in this day and age. Not only has the digital revolution transformed the way we interact, work, and binge-watch our favorite shows, but it has also created a plethora of options for individuals to flex their financial muscles and earn wealth from the comfort of their own homes.

Imagine yourself lounging in your favorite jammies, sipping a cup of steaming hot coffee, equipped only with your laptop and an incredible ability to understand stock market trends. This

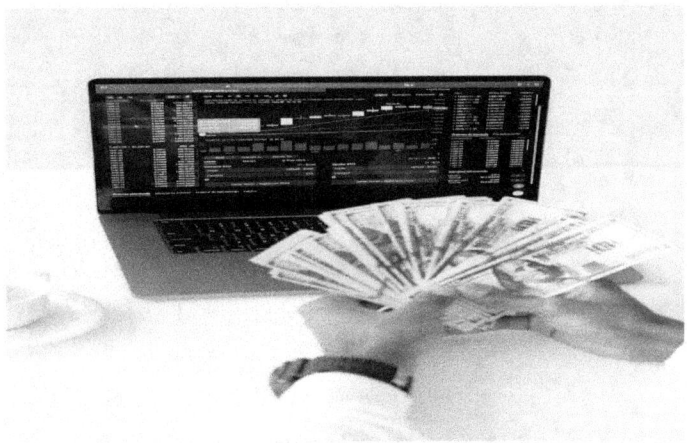

is not a fantasy; it is the reality of online investing. The world of finance has become more accessible to ordinary people like you and me with the introduction of internet investing platforms and trading instruments. And believe me when I say it's a game changer!

Unless you've been living under a rock, you've probably heard some startling news regarding the stock market, inflation, and interest rates. The good news is that this enormous economic upheaval has generated opportunities for astute investors.

The essential phrase here is "smart investors." There are numerous methods for accumulating riches. Long-term investing is preferred by some. Some people prefer to ride the trends via swing investing. Day trading is popular among thrill seekers. There are advantages and disadvantages to each, but the bottom line is that if you haven't considered being the master of your financial destiny, now might be a good time.

Clearly, there is Investing is a method of increasing your wealth through time. It entails investing money in assets such as stocks, bonds, mutual funds, or real estate with the belief that their value will rise and generate a return on your investment. While there are no guarantees in investing, it can be a great tool to build long-term wealth and achieve your financial objectives.

How to Begin Investing

The possibility of big returns is one of the most compelling motivations to invest. Stocks have historically produced an average yearly return of roughly 10% over the long run. This indicates that a $10,000 investment in a diverse stock portfolio may be worth $100,000 in 20 years. Bonds, which are regarded as less risky than stocks, have delivered an annual return of roughly 5% over the same time period. While these returns are not guaranteed and will fluctuate from year to year, they can be a potent instrument for long-term wealth accumulation.

The power of compound interest is another advantage of investing. When you earn interest on your investment, you reinvest it, which allows you to earn even more interest. This compounding impact can greatly increase your returns over time. For example, if you put $10,000 in a mutual fund with an annual return of 8%, your investment will be worth around $46,000 after 20 years. If you reinvest your dividends and let your investment grow, it might be worth more than $90,000 in the same time frame.

Investing can also serve as an inflation hedge. Inflation is the progressive rise in the price of goods and services over time, which can reduce the purchasing power of your money. You can potentially keep ahead of inflation and protect your purchasing power by investing in assets that are predicted to appreciate in value over time.

Investing Risks

Investing, by definition, involves risks. A multitude of factors, including market conditions, firm performance, and economic trends, can cause asset prices to change. It is critical to diversify your investments and avoid putting all of your eggs in one basket. This is investing in a variety of assets, such as stocks, bonds, and real estate, rather than relying on a single type of investment.

Investing might also necessitate a substantial amount of research and understanding. It's critical to understand the risks and have a plan in place for your assets. If you're not sure where to begin or where to invest your money, speaking with a financial advisor who can walk you through the process may be beneficial.

Finishing Up

To summarize, investing can be a great tool for building long-term wealth and achieving financial objectives. While there are no guarantees in investing, the potential for large profits, the power of compound interest, and the ability to hedge against inflation make it an appealing alternative for many investors. However, it is critical to understand the dangers and approach investing with a well-informed and diverse plan.

CHAPTER 7

Leveraging Automation and Technology

"Reducing administrative hours frees up employees to do more creative and critical work." For example, we use Zapier to send payments and refunds to a specific Slack channel, freeing up internal teams to communicate with clients and decide how to best spend the company's budget. Similarly, we automate routine activities such as weekly employee self-assessments to automatically report to a spreadsheet, allowing managers to spend more time coaching and assisting teams and less time gathering and organizing data.

We make it a point to explain to our staff that we have faith in their abilities to do these jobs and want to make the greatest use of their time. By automating these systems, we can cut delays and errors while also giving our employees more room to invent and innovate. Most employees are relieved to be rid of monotonous tasks, especially during busy weeks or seasons."

2. Automate onboarding administration "

Creating a world-class employee onboarding program is a primary People Ops objective at ClickTime. Excellent onboarding not only reduces ramp time but also prepares new recruits for success in ways that benefit our retention, profitability, and revenue. We designed a Zapier link with Google Calendar to automate three weeks' worth of scheduling in seconds, allowing us to spend our time on producing onboarding content rather than scheduling, paperwork, and other administrative tasks that may bog us down. Furthermore, we have automated the collection of paperwork and signatures via our HRIS. This has saved us hours of time every hire and allowed us to focus our efforts on high-impact onboarding."

3. Adopt automation for social media recruiting "

Recruiting has never been more difficult. To remain competitive and top-of-mind with the best applicants, HR and talent acquisition professionals must be strategic in what they automate in order to not only save time but also attract exponentially more and higher-quality prospects. Hiring is a social process, therefore investing in the appropriate automation that can extend your recruitment reach and messaging without sounding robotic is critical.

Social media recruiting is one of those areas where automation can make or break your recruiting approach. If you get it wrong, you could be adding months of work to your team while missing out on the talent you deserve. But get it right, and you may save almost a thousand hours per year while simultaneously attracting a large number of applicants—time better spent by actively (and humanely) engaging with prospects during the hiring process."

4. Make candidate outreach and follow-up automated.

"Repetitive, manual processes like candidate outreach and follow-up can benefit from technology and automation." Recruiters spend a lot of time and mental energy manually sending out follow-up emails to job candidates: setting a reminder, drafting the email, and maybe customizing it a little. This could take at least five minutes per email.

Hiring teams can use recruiting automation solutions to set up interaction sequences for open opportunities that go out at a specified candace. This one process can save recruiters hours of time per day, allowing them to focus on interviewing and obtaining a sense of what candidates are truly thinking—something that only people can do."

5. Determine which tasks can (and cannot) be automated "

Automation can help your employees by taking on tasks that don't require a human touch, allowing them to focus on those that do." However, it is critical to decide which jobs can be automated. Tasks that must be completed more than once and in the same manner each time are ideal candidates for automation. Email marketing and reminders are two examples of communication duties that can be readily scheduled and automated. In some circumstances, content creation can be automated, but it must be reviewed and approved by a human employee. Talk to your employees for thoughts on when to automate an activity. They might have good ideas about which chores automation might help them with and which automation can make their jobs more difficult."

6. Automate project status updates "Thanks to project management software and instant status updates, workflow automation has helped us create a better system across every team in our business." We utilize it in everything from human resources and marketing to sales, information technology, and accounting. Many of our contacts have been automated by updating a single project status rather than digging through emails, sending multiple messages, and hope the recipient sees them, which has helped avoid costly delays and performance issues. Furthermore, our staff is more cohesive than ever. We're seeing them become more engaged with their work and go above and above for our clients, with automation alleviating much of their workload."

7. Communicators' inclusiveness and sentiment analysis

"While communication technologies have advanced significantly, creating engaging and appropriate content is still something that people excel at." Traditionally, the creation of communications within an organization was limited to a few employees with the appropriate training and desire. This has been difficult because there are vast untapped sources of subject knowledge. People may be experts in their field, but they are apprehensive of writing and publishing to a large audience. AI-powered inclusion and sentiment analysis is a recent communication automation that I believe will empower content producers in any company. These programs do automated tests on written language and make language suggestions based on whether the phrase is inclusive or exclusive and whether the tone is positive or negative. Over time, these features encourage authors to write in more inclusive, constructive ways, giving them more confidence to contribute."

"Employee burnout is on the rise, and organizations are grappling with how to deal with the next 'pandemic of mental health,' which is having a critical impact on company performance, revenue, and productivity."

The growing emphasis on employee well-being has presented HR departments with both a challenge and an opportunity to strengthen their employee wellness programs and invest in wellbeing technology solutions to make a significant positive impact. Employee productivity and efficiency can be increased by reimagining corporate processes using technology and automation. Organizations can create new processes that include technology into important moments that matter by automating stressful, time-consuming chores, allowing employees to focus on more meaningful activity.

Using technology to improve mental health yields not only significant results, but also a considerable return on value (ROV) through increased productivity and a more seamless employee experience."

"To leverage technology and automation to keep people focused on the work that humans do, leaders must highlight the importance of collaborative intelligence and encourage employees' professional development with 'fusion skills' that allow people to work effectively at the human-machine interface." Companies will increasingly be organized on various sorts of abilities rather than formal job titles in the future, with corporate functions reorganized around the desirable outputs of reimagining processes. People must learn to delegate jobs to new technologies in the same way that doctors learnt to trust technology by reading X-rays or MRIs. Employees must be able to teach intelligent agents new abilities and educate them to perform well within AI-enhanced processes, such as knowing how to ask the most rewarding questions to an AI agent. Finally, staff must guarantee that organizations' AI systems be used appropriately, that is, that they do not breach legal or ethical bounds."

CHAPTER 8

Scaling Your Digital Empire

"How do I scale my empire?" If you've ever wondered this, keep reading to discover about the top 5 problems that entrepreneurs confront on a daily basis. You might just find out what's holding you back.

"Scalability" refers to your company's ability to cope with, and even prosper in the face of rapid growth.

If your company can maintain or even improve productivity, efficiency, and overall performance while growing, it is scalable.

However, expecting the business to develop by just increasing the top line is a trap that many (now) experienced entrepreneurs have fallen into. If you don't lay a solid foundation for scale, the house of cards you're building will undoubtedly collapse.

Building a firm that can scale and profitably requires a combination of techniques, ranging from your unique selling point to how you set up a team to deliver. It may appear to be an impossible endeavor, but businesses do it all the time, and it can be distilled down to just a few things to get right to offer you the best chance of success.

1 Choosing the Gap

Are you really here to construct yet another mouse trap?

When I engage with a business looking to scale, the first question I ask is, "What makes you unique in the market?"

I'm usually met with a few 'umms' followed by a 'we really care about the results we produce for our clients' or 'we can do the same thing but at a lesser cost' or anything along those lines.

Guess what, I have some good news for you.

Nobody sets out to provide poor service to their consumers.

To remain profitable, that larger firm you left to start your own definitely had to make some tough decisions on customer service.

They most likely no longer have the startup mentality and high-performing crew that you did in your early years.

But they aren't laughing evilly around a table about how they are going to do a bad job and get compensated for it.

Let me tell you where you're headed if you're just going to start another consulting services business doing the same thing everyone else is doing, rebadged, at a cheaper cost and with better services.

High quality usually comes at a higher cost (regardless of what rainbow you've been sold by that low-cost outsourcing business), and low quality means The Dead Zone.

If you want to stand out from the crowd, turn heads, and truly generate scale, you must do something distinctive.

Consider what the market is doing today, where it will go in the next few years, and then identify the gap that needs to be filled.

Even better, understand your purpose and build a company around a fundamental shift you want to bring about and a person or people you want to influence.

This exercise is about developing a brand-led business rather than a skill- or product-led business, as many of us who "leave corporate" do.

Aureus Financial is an excellent example of a brand-led business that is motivated by a desire to change the way an industry operates. Jackson, Sam, and the team have spent a significant amount of time understanding the industry shift they want to create and then building a business around it.

It's a fundamental shift from how you're used to building a business, but it's one that will keep you relevant and competitive for years to come.

2 Increase income while retaining profit

OMG, you're making money like crazy! Revenue is increasing, and you're expanding your team.

But with a large team comes a lethal overhead.

Remember, revenue is vanity, profit is sanity, and cash flow is reality.

As the company grows, so does the team, and the overheads. And in ways you might not have expected.

A larger team may necessitate more non-billable administrative personnel and managers. It may also necessitate larger and more expensive office space in order to create the cool agency vibe that will attract top talent. Not to mention that recruiting has evolved into a major project with its own cost center.

We like Vinny Antonio's statement, which John Hall shares in his Forbes article on the challenges of fast-growing companies.

"It's nearly a full-time job keeping track of who owes you what and who owes you what, and then prioritizing those payments." All the while, you're pushing for more expansion, but that comes with additional costs, most notably your executive team."

"Utilization" has another, possibly more insidious, impact on profit.

A fancy-sounding term for "how much time your team spends on the bench versus delivering actual billable work."

It becomes more difficult to keep the team scheduled into client work and hold them accountable as the team grows. As the workload increases, people may become overwhelmed by indecision and end up delivering less.

Project management and resource planning are somewhat dry topics, but they are critical to the successful management of a business.

You must structure your client delivery to maximize margin, then closely monitor that margin. Similarly, you must have a clear understanding of your team's capacity and optimize their schedule in order to reduce that overhead, non-productive cost in your organization.

A team that spends half of its time on the bench, blown up to scale, is a huge drain on your bottom line and is frequently where the house of cards collapses.

Fortunately, we cover this in a more entertaining manner in our blog, "The Top 5 metrics every agency must measure for growth."

Finally, if you are not monitoring your costs, keeping projects profitable, and the team optimized, you will be missing out on a huge opportunity to generate profit that can be fed back into growth (or rewarding yourself for the hard work), and at worst, you will see your hard work come crashing down due to poor cash flow.

3 Empower a team to work for you

If you want to scale a services business, it goes without saying you'll need to hire a team to deliver for you.

But simply hiring and expecting they'll do things like you do is a trap that will lead to certain collapse.

One of the reasons you may have started your business to begin with is the fact that you are good.
Like really good.
You're a creative marketing genius with a talent for inspiring a team that genuinely knows what your clients are going through day to day.

Sales are a breeze since you connect at such a deep level with your clientele. You've been there. Delivery is easy as you harness years of experience and (let's face it) hustle above and above the call of duty.
But when it comes time to scale, there's a bit of a dilemma.

We haven't mastered cloning yet.

Sure, we've cloned a sheep or three, but we're some way off building an army of you to expand the business upon.

And as the business increases in complexity you'll realize you can't master every discipline.

There's no way of getting around it: there are going to be some things that you'll have to let go of and trust others to handle for you.

I've noticed business owners tend to fall into one of two groups — they either regard delegation as a spot of 'two up' and hope the team will do the right thing, or go full on control freak and micro-manage. Neither strategy works in the long run.

The difficulty you have is that there's no established technique, no basic template, no single go-to system for everyone to follow.

You might begin to notice things slide through the gaps like work being incomplete or released before going through the required steps of editing and approval. This obviously leads to some clients becoming disappointed.

Losing credibility at this stage of the business game would surely be a big blow and a tough (but not impossible!) setback to comeback from.

You have to systemise your business to empower others to work for you.

But what does that even mean?

Well you cannot expect a team to just deliver work 'like you do'. You have to provide them the actions and the tools to follow to produce the client experience you want.

It's all about systems – individuals, following a process, using a platform to get a goal.

Think about the customer experience you want to create – what are all the steps required for someone else to duplicate this without you being engaged.

Then, work out who will deliver each aspect of that experience - what are the duties, abilities and expertise required to do sales, or a particular part of delivery.

Then a platform is your multiplier. For sure you can accomplish just about anything using paper and pen or a spreadsheet, but once you get into more advanced technology platforms you can start to automate parts of your organization and sharply lower the cost of work while increasing the volume of work that's being provided.

The problem with technology is that it has one other incredibly crucial benefit — data. Or, more specifically, reporting on that data to provide you with the insights you need to make sound decisions that will drive your growth strategy.

4 Understand your numbers.

Do you have the impression that your company is a black box?

Making informed judgments about marketing strategy, sales procedure, project delivery, and personnel planning is critical to scaling your organization.

Your tiny staff and client portfolio are expanding quickly, and it's becoming increasingly difficult to keep track of every single job.

Hopefully, you've followed our earlier recommendations and systematized your firm to the point where you're convinced the team can generate results for you. But that is only the first step.

It is vital to be able to measure and hold your team responsible to your company's key success indicators.

Furthermore, as previously stated, your profit margin is at considerable risk of declining as you expand the workforce. Being able to identify and address problems as they arise is critical to preserving profitability - and hence your capacity to continue increasing the team.

Knowing what metrics to track and developing habits in your team to enter data and review results on a regular basis is an important element of scaling your business.

To make things easier for you, we've compiled a list of key metrics to monitor in our latest blog

,

5 Technology, the Great Multiplier.

The next 'Industrial Revolution' of our time is technology automation, whether it is software and workflow, robotics, or advanced Artificial Intelligence.

Everything we've talked about so far has been basic, solid business practice. Entrepreneurs have been identifying market gaps, automating procedures, focusing on profit, and tracking their figures since the dawn of time.

We will witness a convergence of social and technological developments over the coming decade that will practically transform the way we function as a society.

Businesses who capitalize on this massive shift today will be the market leaders tomorrow.

And it's no longer an expensive prospect.

In fact, sales and project delivery systems that were previously exclusively available to major organizations and costing multiple $100,000s to set up are now available on a monthly license for less than $100/month!!

These platforms provide numerous advantages, including the ability to work from anywhere (potentially reducing office costs or even traditional regional' sales boundaries), automate mundane tasks that used to consume your team's time, and produce sharp decision-making insights across massive data sets that would normally take months to process.

But it might feel like a minefield figuring out which technological platforms are best for your company, how to integrate them, and finally how to properly set them up with the workforce.

Fortunately, there are others who can assist you, including yours truly at Scale My Empire (shameless plug).

In just a few years, we'll see Artificial Intelligence (AI) become highly familiar and infiltrate every aspect of our industry. AI can literally transform the game of business and free us up to focus on distinctively human activities like exploration, creativity, and relationship building if we don't hand over the keys to the nukes.

We will align our work with our mission.

The future is definitely exciting, and those who capitalize on the multiplying potential of digital platforms will be both highly scalable and at the helm of the next corporate revolution.

CHAPTER 9

Protecting and Growing Your Wealth

Everyone wishes to accumulate and pass on their wealth to future generations.

But where do you begin?

How do you avoid spoiling your children in the process?

How should wealth be transferred in order to cut taxes and empower the next generation?

We give practical insights in our Generational Wealth Roadmap that you can start implementing today to develop generational wealth. Our mission is to provide a foundation for your family's potential, freedom, and generosity.

The finest tax solutions frequently include transferring assets to the appropriate legal structure and watching them grow over time. Transferring your assets to the next generation frequently involves years of planning and execution by a team of professionals. Over time, family partnerships, trusts, LLCs, and other entities can amplify the impact of investment performance.

In collaboration with your legal and tax experts, our wealth management team evaluates your present structure and makes recommendations to optimize your results.

Estate Planning for the Next Generation

Estate planning is important not only for tax purposes, but also for laying the financial groundwork for the future generation. Our wealth management team collaborates with attorneys and tax specialists to create and implement an estate plan to meet your wealth transfer goals. Estate planning frequently begins with tax objectives, but it is also an excellent opportunity to empower the next generation of your family and leave a legacy in the community. It is not the end, but rather the start of the next generation.

Excellent estate and wealth transfer strategies, like tax planning, can take years to develop and implement. Our experts will work with you to assist you make financial decisions. Then, in collaboration with your solicitors, we construct and administer entities such as trusts or partnerships to carry out your strategy.

Are you ready to collaborate with us?

3 Easy Steps:

STEP 1: ENGAGE IN A CONVERSATION

We'd like to learn more about you, your family, and your issues. We ask questions during a 20-30 minute introduction call to better understand your condition and aspirations.

If our services are a good fit for your needs, we will schedule a One-Page Plan meeting to go over a few initial insights that are unique to you as well as a proposal for working together.

STEP 2: MEETING FOR A ONE-PAGE PLAN

We provide you with a "One-Page Plan" of recommendations that you can maintain. We frequently discuss major issues right here!

Discuss a workshop proposal to thoroughly cover your retirement, tax, investing, and wealth planning problems.

We give you time to determine if you want to collaborate with us after we have answered all of your questions.

STEP 3: WORKSHOP ON FINANCIAL PLANNING

We gather information and analyse your financial status using digital tools.

We get down and pool our resources to address your most pressing investing, tax, and wealth planning issues.

Make a plan for achieving your objectives and discuss how to carry it out in the future.

personaealt

Personal asset preservation necessitates legal planning, proper insurance, and creditor safeguards.

Consider buy-sell agreements, key person insurance, and proper corporate categorization to protect a business.

Personal wealth can be increased through the use of qualified retirement plans, estate planning, and philanthropy.

Growing and keeping your wealth should be a continuous priority, regardless of your stage of life. These ten suggestions can help you chart a roadmap for your financial future.

Personal wealth preservation

Wealth preservation is a strategy for increasing the value of your assets while leaving a legacy for your family. There are numerous investing programs available, all of which attempt to secure your wealth over time.

1. Put your legal affairs in order.

Every day, bad things happen to good people, so it's critical to create a will in the event of your death. You should also have a living will, sometimes known as an advance medical directive, to ensure that your preferences for medical treatment are followed if you become incapacitated. A durable power of attorney for health care is required so that a designated person can make decisions in situations not covered by an advance directive. Navigate your financial future with the goal of wealth preservation, asset and business protection, and legacy enhancement in mind.

Growing and keeping your wealth should be a continuous priority, regardless of your stage of life. These ten suggestions can help you chart a roadmap for your financial future.

Personal wealth preservation

Wealth preservation is a strategy for increasing the value of your assets while leaving a legacy for your family. There are numerous investing programs available, all of which attempt to secure your wealth over time.

1. Put your legal affairs in order.

Every day, bad things happen to good people, so it's critical to create a will in the event of your death. You should also have a living will, sometimes known as an advance medical directive, to ensure that your preferences for medical treatment are followed if you become incapacitated. A durable power of attorney for health care is required so that a designated person can make decisions in situations not covered by an advance directive.

2. Always, always, always insure. Check your insurance coverage.

To provide for your family, consider life insurance for income replacement and goal funding, such as a college education for young children. You can save money by combining term and permanent insurance.

Another necessity is disability insurance; throughout the course of a career, a person is more likely to suffer from a long-term disability than to die.

Liability umbrella insurance provides additional liability coverage to protect assets, wages, and investments from damages that exceed the coverage provided by existing policies.

3. Keep an eye on your accounts.

There are many bad actors, and data breaches are getting increasingly regular. Monitor your credit score and perform an annual credit check to keep them at bay and preserve your identity.

4. Create creditor safeguards.

Trust is frequently used to protect assets from creditors. Because state laws differ, it is best to get legal counsel.

Business model thinkers consider the art of the possible. They comprehend the function of technology in their company's business and industry, as well as adjacent industries, in order to provide a larger context for the impact of technology on business and revenue growth.

Keeping the company safe

A successful business is a valuable asset that can support you and your family. It is critical to protect its operations.

5. Planning for business succession.

It's not uncommon for a business owner's heirs to be uninterested in or unfit to manage the company. Families with a business may want to explore a buy-sell agreement that specifies how co-owners or co-shareholders can purchase your shares when you retire or die. Arrangements can take many different forms and may include a cross-purchase, redemptions, and/or life insurance.

6. Select key person insurance.

Another rationale for life insurance is to lessen the likelihood of a firm failing due to the death of a key employee.

CHAPTER 10

Sustaining Long-Term Success

There are no shortcuts to achievement since success is the accumulation of interest. It is the sum of numerous tiny efforts over time. Like most people, you have dreams that you hope will come true one day. However, without clarity, preparation, and dedication, they are likely to remain just that. The road from dream to reality is difficult. Not everyone is cut out for it.

However, by examining some of the approaches and strategies employed by individuals who have succeeded, it is possible to gain an advantage.

The four approaches listed below can assist you in achieving long-term, sustainable success. They accomplish this by assisting you in developing lofty goals, strict deadlines, and the attention required to execute on a daily basis.

1. Use this three-step method to establish specific goals.

It's easier than ever to lose sight of our ambitions these days. Because distractions are the most common issue that most people confront when attempting to attain achievement.

Our culture is designed to keep us distracted. From the never-ending 24-hour news cycle to notifications that prompt us to check our phones more than 200 times every day.

If you're a creative person, you're likely to have a wide range of interests. Reading the latest blog post, watching the latest TV show, or scouring the internet for ideas are all frequent ways to waste many hours each day.

To keep from wandering, we must be clear about our objectives. But, maybe more crucially, we must understand what our aims are not.

2. Assign a specific deadline to each target.

When most people set a goal, one of the biggest mistakes they do is not giving it an endpoint. You're just dreaming if you don't have a deadline to work toward.

Give each of your top five goals a deadline by which they must be completed. You'll note that this forces you to be specific about what you're attempting to accomplish.

This year, one of my goals was to "lose weight." But that was too ambiguous.

I had to give myself a specific target by giving myself an endpoint.

So "get in shape" became "lose 9.5kg by August 30th." I set a deadline for myself and was able to transform a vague goal into a concrete one.

A set deadline creates a sense of urgency. It also gives shape to your timeline, allowing you to plan what steps to take and when. Because reality can be messy, it's okay if your endpoint shifts if something unexpected occurs. But before you can begin, you must first stake your claim.

3. Set lofty and memorable goals for yourself.

This may seem counterintuitive, but a 100% success rate is a bad thing. A good goal is one that is ambitious enough to require 60-70% achievement.

This is a technique known as stretch goals,' and it is used by some of the world's most successful people. Google, the world's second most valuable company, requires its employees to set stretch goals for each quarter. Here's how they explain it:

If you're routinely achieving 100% of your goals then you are not being ambitious enough. You're leaving wins on the table and playing it safe. This isn't a school exam where you'll be awarded for getting the proper answer to each question. You've got to think bigger than you're comfortable with in order to develop 'moonshots'.

By creating goals that are slightly overly ambitious you drive yourself to perform at a higher level. Sometimes that means you need to settle for only achieving 70%. But at other times you'll hit the ball out of the park and surprise yourself.

If you don't establish huge goals it's hard to acquire big wings

It's impossible to score if you don't know where the goalposts are.

I've been writing for almost a year now. In that time I've almost every day. However, a lot of it was wasted time since I didn't know what I was doing it for. It's taken me almost 365 days to figure out why I'm writing, what my aspirations are and when I want to attain them by. Now I've got a framework to operate in and it just makes my daily life lot easier. I'm also getting far higher returns on the energy I'm investing. Because I now have a clear path to follow.

It's a lot easier to strike your target when you know what you're going for.

Whatever your notion of success is, you'll need a strong foundation to build it on. These approaches will assist you in doing so. The rest is a matter of having the foresight not to rush, the discipline to remain consistent, and the focus to keep going.

4. Limit yourself to only six tasks per day (you'll get more done).

Things can get chaotic when you're trying to hold down a career, raise a family, and launch a side business. Even if you just work one day a week, the list of daily tasks can be daunting. However, 'being busy' is a definite method to never get anything done.

'You are well aware that being busy is a trap and that being busy is a lie. Please do not use the 'busy' card.' Seth Godin's

We can all relate to feeling stretched at times. Being busy, on the other hand, is a result of not having a defined framework with which to tackle your workload. Because you only have so many hours in the day, it's critical to limit your activities to only the most vital ones.

You should now have a clear set of aggressive goals with a specific timeline. The next stage is to take at least one action toward making goals a reality each day. The Ivy Lee approach is one of the simplest and most successful ways to accomplish this.

In order of importance, write down the six most important things you need to do today.

Begin with the first and only move on to the second when it is finished.

Work your way through the entire list in this manner, completing as many chores as possible.

Make a list for tomorrow at the conclusion of the day. Carry over any unfinished chores and add new ones until you have six again.

It's one of the most basic methods to productivity I've seen. However, it has also enabled me to 10x my output. There will be no multitasking. There will be no emailing in the middle of the day. There are no distractions. Only do one thing at a time.

What's fantastic about this method is that it pushes you to consider carefully which chores go on your list and in what order. You should always ask yourself if a task contributes to or detracts from your five goals. The latter should be avoided. Give priority to the former.

Conclusion

"In conclusion, keep in mind that adaptability is essential in this rapidly changing digital landscape." Accept change, stay curious, and keep looking for new ways to make money. With the principles explained in this book, you'll be able to confidently navigate the digital world and leave a lasting legacy of success. Now, go forth and let the Digital Wealth Formula be your path to a prosperous and financially free future!"